NOTES FROM THE DRY COUNTRY

NOTES FROM THE DRY COUNTRY

POEMS BY

ELLEN ARONOFSKY COLE

MAYAPPLE PRESS 2019

Published by   Mayapple Press
                362 Chestnut Hill Road
                Woodstock, NY 12498
                mayapplepress.com

ISBN 978-1-936419-87-6
Library of Congress Control Number 2019930172

ACKNOWLEDGEMENTS

Bellevue Literary Review; District Lines; The Little Patuxent Review; Pulse, Music from the Heart of Medicine; Tailfins and Sealskins: An Anthology of Water Lore (Three Drops Press, 2016); *The Washington Post Magazine* online edition

Several poems are reprinted from *Prognosis*, a chapbook by Ellen Aronofsky Cole (Finishing Line Press, 2011)

I want to express my deepest thanks to my family for their unending love, support and patience, especially my husband, Brian Cole, my daughters and their husbands, Becky Cole Stone and Devin Stone, Laura Cole Riley and Adam Riley, my siblings, Wayne Aronofsky and Sharon Aronofsky Weltman, and to the never-fading memory of my most beloved parents and older sister, the late Julius and Molly Aronofsky, and Barbara Aronofsky Latham. I love you all.

Cover art by Margaret Georgiann. Photo of author on cover by Becky Stone. Photo in Author Bio by Brian Cole. Book designed and typeset by Judith Kerman with titles in Lucida Sans and text in Calfornian FB.

Contents

The country of the innumerable dead was empty. No tree or blade of grass grew in the stony earth under the unsetting stars. "I am thirsty," Arren said, and his companion answered, "Here they drink dust."

Ursula K. LeGuin, The Farthest Shore

I

Excision

1. The Cancer

I've named my breasts
Titania and Peas-blossom
my sister said

Peas-blossom is never any trouble
but Titania is a real drama queen
hogging all the attention

she hasn't even noticed
how she's become entangled
in Bottom's arms

how he keeps sucking down
grapes   belching
his spittle smeared across her chest

he doesn't know
he's about to be
excised

2. Who will not die

Aunt Norma said if you dream
of a child someone will die

but in my dream
the baby was small and shy as quail

unnamed
her heart beat like the sun

Grandpa's ghost toasted us
with apricot schnapps

Grandma Celia fed us hot apple slices
bedded on fat yellow noodles

My cousin Tom snapped pictures
like he did years ago at our wedding
Brian, his white wedding suit
dusted with sugar

tipping cake into my mouth,
Tom focusing on fingers, lips

everything extraneous
cut out

3. Everything is a knife

The phone slashes my ears
Your voice drips out the earpiece
My tongue lies in my mouth
thick as a tumor
I would pull it out before I tell you this news

But words grow in my belly
quick as fungus
climb my bones
I cannot keep them still

I am like the maiden in a fairy tale
when I open my mouth birds fly out
I try to call them back
but they have flown to a dry country

where neither blood nor water flows

Lightheaded

as I so often am
when leukemia fevers sweep over me
I fail to notice when I begin to rise,
feet bidding the floor good-bye,

I say, *Brian*, but you,
your eyes shut,
Beethoven's *Moonlight Sonata*
whispering in your earphones,

do not see me wink out the window
like lamp light, the lawn glittered
with glow-worms, echoed above
by the stern slow music of stars.

I blow northeast carried
by prevailing winds, pass
like fair weather into morning,
drift over Newfoundland.

The sea is frozen into strange shapes,
waves solidified. Spray arcs like mermen
caught in the arctic air, the sky's blue bell
pinched into a funnel, soars above my head.

A young bull seal, his head bashed in,
half-eaten fish held in his mouth, floats
above me. Seal and fish turn their eyes
upward where light tubes into the unknown.

My hair flaps like a mariner's flag.
My mouth, agape, still holds your name.

Guano

after Anton Checkhov

Once there were three sisters
who all had cancer.
The eldest two had leukemia,
the youngest a small malignancy
in her right breast.
The odds against this happening
were astronomical.

Of course they weren't all sick
at the same time. Sharon
had a quick lumpectomy
and four short months of chemo.
Barbara was diagnosed and
died twenty-five years ago.
Terrible luck, Ellen said.
Doctors can cure that now.

Moscow was not far
but the girls didn't know.
Outside an unusual July snow
dropped thirty-six inches
on the Russian countryside
and a drift of seagulls
blew in from the north.

The Scream

At that moment, among the trees nearby, a horn rang out. It rent the night like fire on a hilltop. "Awake! Fear! Fire! Foe! Awake!"
J. R.R. Tolkien

She woke and screamed,
Her head rang like a horn,
clanged like a warning bell,
pealed *Fire! Fear! Foe!*
She burrowed under covers
but screams pumped out.
Daughters sheltered against the wall.
Screams caught the chandelier,
sent it spinning.
Her neighbors sat up in their beds,
smashed their heads on walls.
Her parrot broke its beak against cage bars.
Her husband cupped her face,
said *hush.*
She whimpered.
Everything was ice.

Shadow Sister

She was born when I was born,
was with me in the womb
and dropped unseen
from between my mother's legs
when the doctor slid me from the birth canal
and held me for my first breath.

She walked with me when I
was twelve and my puppy Count Down
was hit by a car, releasing
his shadow pup to run free.
Why do things die? I asked my father.
He said, *Don't worry about it, Sweetness.*

But I kept dreaming about the fish
I caught in Miller's Pond and put
in an old aquarium, how they floated
belly-up after a few days
casting their small shadows
on the glass floor.

And I know she is here with me,
my precise shape and size,
pacing the cancer ward,
peering out the window at the gulls
and snow geese gathered
in the parking lot below.

In the Lobby at Johns Hopkins

I see a baby with no face.
Her eyes are lidless.
Her nose, a hole.
Her mouth, a lipless gash.

Her father tenderly wipes her chin.
Her hands, furled like flower
buds, push through the sleeves
of her pink fleece sweater.

I can't forget her. I'm in the infusion
chair. Tubes snake my arms.
I dream of owl babies. They perch
on IV poles, crowd onto cots,

fill the halls. Doctors rush by.
The owlets neither eat nor sleep.
They have no feathers.
They do not blink.

Fear Mice Make a Movie

What is your birth date? asks the nurse
April 16, 1950   I say

She checks the barcode on the IV bag
Fear Mouse looses itself from my stomach
runs up my spine

If I die will I be razored out of the picture
fluttering like a sliver of celluloid
to the cutting room floor
that date disappearing altogether

Slik-slak
Another Fear Mouse runs up my spine
Another

Hamster Heart jogs in his wheel
Beats 110 times per minute

Fear Mice slip on their ruffled skirts
Sing   *Girls, do you know that you'll die*
              Never ask me why why

They link arms   kick   Their high heels puncture
precise circles inside my skull

Hamster Heart beats 200 times per minute

Fear Mice turn their backs   flip up their skirts
They kick up plastic snippets
Time confetti fills the air
              1956 I have measles on my birthday
              1980 Brian and I marry
              2009 Doctor Gore says *you couldn't find 100 people*
              who have the same disease as you

Fear Mice sing
              You will die-eee I-ee die–ee die-eee

Hamster Heart slips out of his wheel
Beats 50 times per minute

Fear Mice grasp each other's shoulders
Sway
Hum Brahms Lullaby

Hamster Heart beats 10 times per minute
Hamster Heart shuts his eyes

Slik-slak
April 16 disappears from time.

Cancer Blues

Doctor, Doctor, I'm feeling wrong.
Doc, I'm feeling something's wrong.
Gonna come see you, won't be long.

Something's growing that shouldn't be there.
Something's growing that never was there.
Cut it out, it's given' me a scare.

Chemo's making me sick as a dog.
Damn poison makes me sick as a dog.
Tummy's jumping like a love-sick frog.

Walking slow with Mama's cane.
Well, I'm walking slow with Mama's cane.
Doctor, cut me open again.

I'm getting stringy, getting thin.
Yeah, getting stringy, getting thin.
Need some clothes they can bury me in.

Blue Clown

pokes his head
out of the hospital cabinet
with his sad-face on
and the small whisperings
from under the bed
cannot be understood.
Time pleats like a fan
so you are there
and there and there
like an old movie show.
I do not see you move
from place to place.
The doctor is speaking
but I cannot unravel
what he says;
his voice tangles
with the whispers
under the bed.
I know you are here
but I cannot remember
where you
are sitting or what
you said.
Morphine pulls
my eyes shut
as if two moths
heavy with sun
have settled
over them.

In Isolation at the Sidney Kimmel Cancer Center

Only the nurses kept me company at night.
The long window on my left was a black funnel
sucking heat out of the room, dumping it into
Baltimore. The nurses appeared in my room masked,

wore paper robes to protect me from germs.
The cold shook me in my bed. I begged them to stay
and talk, for heat packs to warm my chest. Neela
offered to assist me to the commode, then vanished

on her rounds. I told Tonia I couldn't stop thinking
about what might happen to me next. She said
she'd ask the Attending to prescribe a tranquilizer,
maybe Ativan, then she too disappeared.

Only Leah slipped back to see me when she was done
answering urgent calls. Leah, the orthodox Jew, who wore
a turtleneck under her scrubs for modesty, who showed me
how to wrap a scarf around my newly bald head. She offered

to rub my back, and when I said I couldn't stop wondering
what death might be like, told me she was worried too, because
she was having an affair, and couldn't stop, even though
it was a sin. I rolled over, careful not to dislodge the tubes

that bound me to the bed, winced when my bird bones
pressed into the plastic pad. She rubbed my back, my calves,
the soles of my feet. I closed my eyes, let her voice
block out the buzz of the IV, and pretended she was my friend.

Pigs

I wake laughing from a dream—
a tree blooming with pigs.
Remember when Laura dreamed

of a pig-tree when she was six?
How we laughed? I ask, and you
try so hard to smile you wince.

The nurse hangs morphine
on my IV. Chemotherapy
has seared my throat, blistered

the mucosa in my mouth.
I decide no more pudding.
No more broth.

My doctor says two things—
You have to eat.
You have to stay strong.

I do neither. I curl onto my side,
wish to suck my thumb.
Patients march past my door

walking their IV poles as if
they were large pets. I push
the button for more morphine.

Pigs drift down from the ceiling
like pink balloons,
settle against my chest.

The Voice in My Head Is the Same

When I was six standing in line
with the rest of the first grade
my guts twisted and released a stench
so foul I could not hide it
from anyone who stood near
and my underpants grew sticky and warm

and one of the second graders lined up
on my right said, *Pee-yoo. The first grade stinks.*
and the voice in my head called me
every bad name it knew
and I pretended I was in my mother's arms
as she washed the nasty mess
off my backside and whispered
This was not your fault.

Five decades later with C-diff spawning
inside my intestines, too weak to reach
the commode two steps from my bed
I push the call button for the nurse
who does not come in time

I lie in an evil-smelling pool
and the voice says *Well, what's the matter
with you, you can't hold it in?*
and the nurse comes in and lifts
me off the bed as if I were light

as a dry stick, a soiled infant of fifty-nine,
and sets me on the commode too late
and I pull the blanket off my bed
to cover the goose bumps
spreading like a rash over my thighs.

I do not wish to write about you

but my mind's a landfill
   overflowing with your breath

your body a cold weight
   layered over mine

Laura and Becky chat by my bedside
   think me asleep

The IV pump drowns out
   the beloved voices on the other side

of the steel bar that rims my bed
   Darling Darling   you sing

You weigh exactly the same
   as my 59 years

Your scythe leans against the wall
   you dive down my throat

rattle your warning into my belly
   You bloom only after fire

has demolished the forest
   Your roots shoot through six floors

maternity   pediatrics   nephrology
   cardiology   intensive care

Even under this great building
   there is dirt

Which Is No Elegy

Dogs are usually dead
in my dreams   so when I rush
to the other house
the one I forgot we owned

the one hidden under the railroad bridge
where the river swelled
without explanation
and submerged our neighborhood

and when the waters withdrew
the house reappeared
its shingles blistered and worn
thin as my skin after weeks of radiation

and I stumble and swish
through puddles that circle
the front stoop   mud and sludge
swirl up with every step

and I remember   just then
as I climb the stained stairs
that once there was a dog in the house
a poodle-corgi mix named George

and I burst open the door
expecting the worst and the padlock
flies off the knob and strikes my chest
above my heart where the port

was implanted for chemotherapy
causing a faint stab and seep of blood
but I hear toenails click across the floor
and even before my ears register hope

his torso thumps against my chest
so hard I feel his fur through the thin cloth
of my hospital gown   the pressure
of his ribs stripes my arms

and his gray tongue protrudes
from his mouth like pressed felt
and I say *my god*
he must be so thirsty

I hold him over the ancient sink
and water pulses out of the tap
tepid and brown
into his quivering mouth

The Bone Marrow Transplant

A woman in Seattle   or maybe
it was a man   walked
into a hospital and allowed them to drill
       a dozen holes in her pelvis
       and suck out marrow

which was expressed to Baltimore
and dripped into me
thick red tomato paste
       brewed in her bones
       infused into mine

where it grew
spreading into the hollow
dead map of bone
       my skeleton a gourd
       scoured of seeds

where it grew   spread
moss carpeting the inside
of a tree   branches blighted but
       refusing to die   the Arborist delighted
       by its continued life

my blood forever changed
to that of my blood sister   blood brother
whose marrow lies   night and day
       at table and in bed
       within me

The Beginning

It was my stomach that woke me,
a sensation so unfamiliar
I pressed my palms against my middle

to catch it, wrists perched
on hipbones, while my ribs imprinted
the bed with their delicate track of bone.

It drove me up. I swung my legs
over the edge, pulled myself into sitting.
An aide wheeled in my morning tray.

Our agreement: he would uncover
my breakfast to shield me
from the nausea that rode the steam.

Oatmeal. Thin, with a sheen of green.
The milk pooling on the edge.
Nubbled, with a look like the kitchen floor.

My lips sealed themselves.
My throat locked its door. Tears
rolled off my cheek, salted the bowl.

Still the feeling drove me.
I grabbed the phone, called Brian.
I said, *Please, bring me food.*

He brought me an egg.
I peeled the porcelain shell.
The white was translucent, perfect.

II

panic attack

i do not want to be this dog
running over ice

no,
i am the ice

frozen between these
two sheets, & fear

rakes my back
judders my guts, my

stomach is hard with it
if i move i'll craze

the sun shoulders into
the room &

One Bird

One bird singing alone before light
has even started leaking beneath
the blinds, my stomach hurts
like hell and I don't notice pain
is creeping up my neck into my jaw
they say in women that means
a heart attack, they say almost
anything could be a heart attack
if you are a woman and think
it's only heartburn, or maybe a twinge
in your shoulder, then bam, you're sorry,
you have to go lie down by the front door
and wait for the ambulance, my heart
keeps beating, *I'm fine, I'm fine,* but I
know these body parts all lie,
how they pretend to be ok
when really you're about to die,
and I remember there's a Xanax
hidden in my second dresser drawer
that my friend Brenda lent me but
what if I take it and I get so sleepy
I forget to call 911, they say
part of your heart can die even if
you survive this time, and that damn
bird keeps singing although the sun
hasn't yet begun to crack the sky
I could try to meditate but can't
think of the mantra I learned in 1972
from the T.M. guru in Worcester, Mass,
so I breathe with the bird, breathe
tcheee-ooop, tcheee-ooop, tcheee-ooop,
one bird singing alone in the night.

A Recipe to Die For

Having nothing better to cook for dinner, I decide
to make a coffin, small, chocolate, with coffee liquor
for a filling. Kahlua and coffin. People will murder

to get this. In fact, it would be a good vehicle
for murder. You could say, "Try this coffin, my dear,"
and the deed would be done. Kahlua would cover

the strychnine or poison of your choice,
which you insert into the coffin with a pastry syringe.
Your victim will be hypnotized by the casket shape,

the sugar flowers, or choose a religious symbol
—a Cross, Star of David, or Crescent and Star.
Or leave it blank, a symbol of nothing to come.

Mold a miniature body out of marzipan
to put inside. Lay it in a bed
of marshmallow, cover with whipped cream.

Or you may use the Petite Chocolate Coffin
for suicide. Ladle on minty Maalox to stave off heartburn.
Your final taste will be sweet, complex,

intoxicating. Quietly compose hymns
while you lick the last sticky bit
of chocolate from your chin.

Angels Who Do Not Love Us

1.

Auntie Ellen, there's a Tyrannosaurs Rex in the back yard,
says Andy.
    No, I say.
He stomps on a row of ants marching over the deck.
Cherry blossoms fill the air with pink.
Something is standing on the lawn,
large, with wings that sweep behind like a huge reptile tail.
Andy is running, running into its small ferocious arms.
I bat away the petals that fill the air, but cannot see.
How will I explain to my sister that her son
was eaten by a T-Rex?

Andy punched me so I bit him, says Becca.
His blood tasted like mud. Look there's something
in the backyard.
    No, I say.
But she too is running through the petals.
Gone.
I race outside, brush petals out of my eyes.
Blinded.
Eaten.
In this part of the poem there is silence.

Petals fall to the ground and the sky is ice blue.

2.

Elizabeth the ex-nun pours herself
another glass of chardonnay.
What if God and Angels are real, but they don't like us?
she asks. The hair on my arm ripples like prairie grass.
I stoop to pick a dandelion, the first I've seen
this season. It stains my fingers yellow.
This morning I saw a picture of a boy,
his arm blasted off by a bomb.
I spill the salt into my coffee,

dump in teaspoon after teaspoon of sugar,
but cannot fix the taste.

3.

.

Why would Angels look like people anyway,
with wings instead of arms?
No, Angels have arms.
Unless Jacob merely dreamed
he grappled with a man-creature
who grasped him with fierce upper limbs.
Maybe all dinosaurs were angels.
A meteor from space announced
it was time to rise to the heavens.
Dinosaurs lifted their wings and flew
lips curling at the apelike creatures
that sloshed out of the mud.

Of course they're still here. We're overrun
with angels. Infested. Consider crows, who study
our trash, take notes on our habits. Lions roar out
dire prophecies while climbing up and down
the golden ladder in the mincing step of the Sphinx.

It's a riddle.
What's the difference between an angel and a fig?
Sweet, says Anteater, who noses
into our earthly business, tattles
back to the Lord. Chewy, says Rat,
sinking his teeth into fruity flesh. Seeds,
says Mosquito, who spits compulsions into our blood,
leaves itchy rounds that whisper secrets to the heavens.

4.

Even vegetables have their say.
Who eats whom, anyway? asks the eggplant,
waiting for the day earth opens and our bodies
will be laid into the dirt.
We thank You for what we are about to receive.

Potatoes grow in their brown burka.
Carrots burrow to Mecca.
Broccoli daven in curly tallit and kipa.
Jack-in-the-pulpit preaches gospel
to a congregation of May apples
who gossip beneath a canopy of leaves,
green fruit poisonous and small.

Once

 there was a girl whose hair
coiled like kudzu over her neck
until her shoulders disappeared
and she moved through the world
like one overrun by leaves.

Once there was a girl whose
 Mother scrubbed her hair until she cried,
scraping her scalp with her fingers
and dousing her with water
until it filled her mouth and nose.

Once there was a girl who
 was afraid to bathe. Her friends said,
*Maybe you're not rinsing the shampoo
out of your hair.* The girl said nothing.
She hadn't washed in three weeks.

Once there was a girl whose hair
smelled of sea rose and yarrow. It eddied
and curled about her face. Her lover
tasted her waves and stayed in her bed
for forty nights and forty days.

Once there was a girl whose hair
fell out. She clipped it short in the cancer ward
but every day her pillow was rough
with itchy strands. When she recovered
her hair grew back thin and gray.

Once there was a girl whose mother
died. Her mother's hair was silver lace draped
down her back. The mortician rouged
her face like an Easter egg. *Doesn't she
look like a queen?* the mortician said.

The Act

My friend told me
under her pillow
last February
it was time
until dawn & she
& I thought of her
when I stood

pills in half
& it seemed to me
into my chest
& I broke out
over coffee & Prozac
she could trust
on its own

she slept with a knife
when she was depressed
in case she felt
& she couldn't wait
found comfort in this
yesterday morning
in the kitchen cutting

with a paring knife
the knife might plunge
if I didn't take care
in a sweat right there
& wondered how
the knife wouldn't act
while she slept

Good God, Girl, Stop with the Death Already

I'm staring at a big gold watch swinging back and forth, murmuring *death, death*. Every poem I write, *boom*, there it is, the skull creeping in, grinning underneath the words.

I whisper, *Please, darling, don't die tonight*, into Brian's healthy sleeping ear. And when Nina in Chekhov's "Seagull" says she always wears black because she's in mourning for her life, I breathe, *Yes*, and vow to heave all my black t-shirts, dresses and pants out the window and dress all in red, because the dead don't wear red.

If there's a gun in Act 1, someone will be dead by Act 3. And there's always a gun. I tell my doctor I can't remember how I knew Nina was going to kill herself. Dr. Oser says, *Don't worry, people with Alzheimer's aren't unhappy. It's their loved ones who suffer.* I promptly forget three more excruciatingly urgent things.

The right side of my face starts twitching and after a week I realize I not only have Alzheimer's, I also have ALS. I write two more sonnets about the Grim Reaper. At night I cry quietly so I won't disturb my beloved.

What do you like better, cremation or burial? I ask him in the morning.

Dr. Oser studies my hands for fasciculations, tells me no ALS today. *How silly of me*, I say, laughing too brightly. Cue to clouds at sunset, "Requiem in D Minor" played by an orchestra of cellos, Prince Hamlet and his flight of angels, a dead mouse moldering in the pantry. A beech tree drops her diseased leaves.

Yom Kippur: A Woman Argues with Her Husband and No One Atones

For Judy

His voice peaks into the scream
of tropical birds   She sinks inside herself

into a walled courtyard   palm trees
silver leaves spiked with orchids

and the flash of macaws too distant to hear
Still she sees the fierce gesture of his arms

She descends further inward
toward marble fountains whose pursed lips

arch water   drops fall
like words divorced of meaning

onto the tense surface of the pond
She is silent as the cobblestone

that lines the path from pool to grass
hedged by thorns and briar bush

There is no entry to this place
Today she is fasting and will not eat

Gardenias border the pool
waxy and inedible

She dives into the water
Now she is a flounder

She huddles against the tile floor
Bottom dweller

No predator will feed on her today
Her eyes gaze up

past the fountains
past the fog of flowers and scent

She sees him
How ugly his face has become

Over his shoulder   outside the window
a goldfinch lights in the ginkgo tree

whose berries promise memory
and smell of vomit

Yellow summer plumage gilds
his plain finch body like fool's gold

Soon he will molt and brown
disappear into the crowd of undistinguished birds

that mob the feeder in the fall
He will not atone for his summer sins

He seizes a berry and scissors a mouthful
into his small beak

disregarding the sour taste
he swallows it whole

Selkie

Moon blooms in my head
drives me over waves and rills
I ride the mother to sea's end
My sisters ribbon the sand
gather where the strand dips low
leap over rock and shell

Moon in my head
I kick away my black seal skin
rise on two stems
toes ten small paddles
to stir the sand
and the mother booms
and splashes and smoothes the beach

And I do not see him
two-legged and man high
Moon in my eyes
Sisters scatter
white bodies round into black pelt
and where is my own?
holder of my own true shape?
Has the mother snatched it away
here where she pulls the tide
into her open face?

And the man
stops digging
and takes my hand
says   selkie come
and I go
for the mother will not take me back
shaped like this for land
and I look at him with black moon eyes
for I have no words

and I go to his house
and here I stay

breathe hot smoke air
and lie with him in his wooden bed

and when the world turns ice
I bear him twins
who nuzzle and suck like any pups
afloat in the winter sea

Moon is a boulder that slides across the icicle sky
and someone has opened the casement wide
the window an eye fringed with night
Through the raised sash
the mother's voice calls
selkie   selkie   selkie of the sea

And I go over the sill
feet push ground away
knees bend and straighten
bend and straighten
until I see the mother
I do not listen to the man
who cries and carries our young
black haired against his pale chest
or is it my old pelt he holds
mangy from months under the sand?

And I do not stop
for the mother sings of quicksilver fish
and my own sweet bed
and moon has laid a ribbon into the octopus deep
so I raise my arms
like human women do

and dive
my hair a twist of black sea grass
my mouth and nose
fill with foam and honey salt
and she draws me in
she draws me in

In Praise of Shallow

your face doesn't get wet
the water only comes up to your boobs
you can wear a t-shirt over your bikini
so you don't have to see *Harris Forever*
tattooed on your midriff in blue
and your mascara won't streak

so you don't look like you're crying
nobody cries at the pool
you don't have to think
about the barbecue last night,
how Harris flirted with Kate's cousin
then they both disappeared

and Sasha saw your hands shake
and drove you home and you kept staring
at her arm where she'd been sawing
at her wrist with a penknife
before she wrote that note last week
about her father

you think maybe you'll pray
to the spirit who lives behind the football field
and everyone chants to it before games
you'll say   *please make Sasha stop hurting herself*
you tried that in church already
it didn't work

the lifeguard is looking at you
you better stop thinking like this
or you'll need Botox before you turn sixteen
you perch on the edge of the pool   your stomach
pooches out even though you didn't
eat anything today but cough drops

and you think   *thank god for nail polish*
Blue Roses   zesty midnight blue
with icy overtones
good thing you used lip liner
this morning before you put on lipstick
so the color won't leach out

Henry the VIII Shops K-Mart

"My G-d, wives are cheap here," Henry Tudor,
Tips, Tricks, and Annulments, *July 14, 1540*

Closing time & the girls & I are standing in our boxes like we always do when this big guy strolls down the aisle & we all start rustling our cellophane because no kidding   it's the real actual king   *Looking for a wife* he says & the clerk nods in our direction   *Right over there Your Majesty* the clerk says   & bows himself out of the aisle fast & we all suck in our stomachs & try to look enticing which isn't easy with the Barbies right next door & there's no competing with them

but we stick out our boobs & jut our hips forward so he'll know our ovaries are loaded & we're primed to push out an heir anytime   but he can't seem to make up his mind   he keeps picking up boxes & putting them back   Anne   Jane   Ann   Katheryn   Catherine & Katherine   he hangs on to Anne Boleyn the longest so we all think she's the one   but he keeps shuffling boxes so we try even harder to look perfect & Katheryn opens her mouth & shows him her tongue

& he goes wild   drooling & all   & rips open her box & throws her in the cart like he's going to ravish her right there   but instead   he keeps ripping open boxes & throwing more & more of us girls into the cart & we all think he has honest to God holes in his basket   when   all of a sudden   he grabs Anne again & slips his hands   around her neck   real gentle like   but instead of a caress   he hooks his thumbs under her chin & starts to push

fear rattles through us like wastepaper blowing down an empty aisle we all know a little pressure like that   we're all the same   our heads will just   pop   off

Cracked Ghazal

My mother holds my pills in the air, says, *I know
what this is.* Her voice cracks.

When I faint in the bathroom they all know
I'm sick. My head hits the john. I never hear it crack.

A scrim hides your face. My lids squeeze together
and I see you through the crack.

Barbara leaves college, runs away to NYC. My father says,
Don't ever come back.

A woman loses her parents. Every day she loses them
again. At night the sun drops into a crack.

We turn 65. What we knew we don't know. Poles flip.
The beginning tarnishes, the ground cracks.

I'm afraid of the dark. Did you know this? At night
I hold onto you, rest my head against your back.

You hunch and my neck wobbles. Moisture
fills my eyes and drips into cracks.

Barbara and I are riding on the El. In the station Daddy
takes my hand. My foot slips in the crack.

In the Days of Trump, I Crave Strawberry Ice Cream

after William Carlos Williams

I forgot how to swallow. I
thought my tongue must have

amnesia. It was as if I'd never eaten
before. I turned the

mess in my mouth but the plums
and pastry crust wouldn't go down. That

was why I twisted away, hoped you were
not looking. I thought I'd lost my mind. In

dreams I devoured steak, bread and butter,
the choicest cherries, emptied the icebox.

At meals I tried to remember which
came first, tongue or throat; when you

turned to the TV, and were
glued to CNN, I probably

bolted from the table. Saving
face was impossible.

For weeks, it was the same. Breakfast,
lunch and dinner. I couldn't forgive

my body. Why was it doing this to me?
I didn't know. My other friends—they

never noticed. Those weeks were
the strangest I've endured. Then the delicious

day that saved me. Something so
simple. My throat relented, accepted sweet.

I could open, I could breathe. So
ice cream. I cling to the pink, the cold.

Blue

I was 25 and driving home from my bad
job to my newish husband, my head
full of silt the way it always was,

and I thought, this is my natural state,
this melancholy. I told my therapist,
a skinny young man named Anthony,

I said, *Everything is wrong except
my marriage.* And Anthony said,
No, that's wrong too.

That was pre-Prozac. Twenty years later
I told my newest shrink, whose name
was Carla, I felt stuffed with rocks,

then dropped in an elevator that fell
straight to floor B3, the lowest
basement parking level. Carla

prescribed Zoloft, then Wellbutrin,
then Lexapro. And a little space opened
in my head, as if some air had bubbled in.

Like 5 AM. It's pitch outside. If you squint
east, you'll see the faintest blue
bleed into the black. It's not the sun.

Not even close. But still,
it's there. That color,
that embryo, that darkest blue.

The Hardest Task

after Adam Zagajewski

It seems it isn't enough to try.
Again, morning is a punch to
the gut. Try to look, to praise.
Here are your feet, your pants. The
task is to rise. You have not been mutilated.
There is oatmeal. There is the world.

III

Transcend

My face a masterpiece in acne
I sank to the lowest adolescent caste
to tread among spazzes and nerds.
I yearned for the back seat of Kevin's sedan.
My Lothario, barely 16, so skinny the rest
of his cohort looked buff, but recast
as Sir Lancelot, his scent
of musky sweat socks was nectar,
his voice from squeak to rant
a tenor angel's bright descant.

First Trimester

There is a secret I wrote in my diary
I will never tell you, although your father
knows. I told him first, even before
I told my best friends Kathy and Dell

and I never told my mother at all.
And when I wrote it, my handwriting
was so tangled and malformed
it fenced in the meaning like barbed wire

looped around fields in spring
so deer will not trespass
and kill what is trying to grow.
And the script in my journal

is so small and uneven no one
can read it, as if I wished to keep
the meaning swaddled in black ink
so it could not cry out.

And when I die, I wish you to destroy
this old journal, dated December 1972
through April 1973, which you will find
on the bottom left shelf in the study,

so you will not be tempted to read
what I don't wish to share.
I had to go to a clinic in those days
in a part of DC I had never been before

because I had no money to speak
of. I know this sounds like a joke,
but I had to go to the basement
to see the doctor

and the other women who waited
wore grey peacoats or denim jackets,
hands thrust into pockets because of the cold,
some with boyfriends or husbands

and some, like me, alone.
On the counter was a vase
of early daffodils. It was only the first week
of March, after all. The receptionist cut

them from her yard and stuck
them here, on the dark avocado linoleum,
where they nodded bravely
in a green soda bottle for everyone to see.

Your father and I were not wed
yet he lay in bed with me and rubbed
my chest in the channel of flesh
that runs from waist to collarbone,

as if he soothed a colicky infant
to sleep, and I shut my eyes
beneath the rubbing
of his large quiet hand.

The Fire

1.

the flames were more beautiful
than you can imagine
the couch haloed with light
smoke beat monstrous wings
against windows   doors
spirit fingers raked the ceiling
                    tiny and far away
 as if I watched through binoculars
turned backwards

I stood in the hallway and gaped
dumb as wallboard
feet planked to the floor
fingers useless as dry sticks

Sammie the Senegal parrot
Tieta the Green Cheeked Conure
Pippi, Laura's guinea pig
died

2.

I lie in bed in the rental house
like a woman sleeping on a dragon
I did it
I turned on the lamp that short circuited
the outlet   lit the couch   and burned the house
I did it
I shake and the bed beneath me
shivers and moans
an old dog with a belly full of ashes and smoke

3.

I dream I'm breakfasting
in the coffee shop at Sanger Harris
with Mom and Grandma Celia.
I say *Forgive me*
The dining table you gave us
your French armchair with flowers
carved on the knees
the geisha doll with the red kimono
all burned
They swivel toward me on their stools
and I see what had been hidden before
their two faces   dear and familiar as my own
charred and flaked away
flat as burned toast
my hands fly to my cheeks
I hear the chink of bone on bone

4.

Light curls into the room
folds into crevices and corners
There are no noises   no birds
I rise and go downstairs
Laura settles the kettle on its small flame
She holds her night in her eyes
The kitchen fills with the scent
of sugar and fruit

My Daughter Laura Is Not an Easy Person to Put in a Poem

She always wears a grin on her front page
but when she hugs you
you can read in the margin
how she once spent three days in bed
because of what her boyfriend did
which she wouldn't explain to her mother
or how she drove 300 miles to Ohio
to rescue her best friend Nora
whose car's engine blew up in Ashtabula
and how she would do the same for you
but only if you were Nora,

and if you read carefully
between the lines you might discover
how Laura cut her arm once
when she was in high school
to see how it would feel
and how Nora
stayed up with her
and they sang Celtic ballads
until the blood stopped
and there was no more pain,

and if you are quick and observant
you'll find a footnote that explains
Laura is not afraid of her mother's
red-bellied parrot Haiku
who has a special affection for biting
people's fingers and toes until they bleed
but Laura will stroke Haiku's beak
until his orange eyes close
and his dry pink tongue sticks out,

and I warn any young person who might
go back to her dark apartment to canoodle
to remember how Laura
mesmerized that bird

with the quick sugared strokes
of her thumb until Haiku
lay on his back in Laura's palm
and preened
the small hairs on her arm
with his fierce sweet beak.

After 2 Weeks of Rain

when sun fills up the room with yellow
I'm so happy I stop cleaning
& start to boogie, singing
Rocky Raccoon checked into a room,
& I'm Back in the USSR all over
the kitchen, my back aching just a bit
& that ankle I've twisted about 800 times
giving me a twinge but now I'm thinking
how my roommate Kathy & me listened
to the White Album every night,
lights out in our dorm room,
blackbird singing at the edge of night,
me thinking of that time we saw them perform
in Detroit & how I screamed as loud
as the girl who ran up the aisle yelling
I touched him! I touched Ringo's thumb!

Babies

I told my mother I did not want any babies
                          I lied
I wanted babies   I wanted a crèche full of babies
I wanted babies
            sweet round babies
Like bowls of m & ms   Like marshmallows
whose roly-poly bodies
you could pour on your face
piles of babies
Babies you could wrap yourself in
like bubble paper   The world could not crack or injure you
because you were wrapped in babies

My husband did not agree

                  We had a big fight
Not about babies
He thought it would be a good idea to pave
the back yard so we wouldn't have to mow any more
Of course we divorced

A few years later I met someone who preferred
living matter to construction material

I fell in love when he told me he was driving
his red 1972 Road Runner to work
                          when he found
his neighbor's cat had been hit by someone's car
and instead of going to work he took Buttercup
                          to the vet   swaddling her in his jacket

He noted how her blood fell like cinnamon balls
to roll beneath her fur until they flattened
                  She cried and bit his arm when he laid her in the car
determined to rescue her
even though he knew what her heart's stain would
                          do to his new white leather seat

After Our House Burned Down

Laura names the rental house Frederique
charmed by shapes carved in the molding

but the curlicues frown at me
Nightmares scurry about
drape my face like webs
I search the bed but find nothing

only our own house
ghost house
burns behind the walls

I feel my way downstairs
grab my journal
write for comfort
I write about Laura

Somehow I conjure her
She bolts from her bedroom
her face stark as 2 am

I saw spiders under my bed   she says
Three spiders   Frederique has spiders

Her lashes are wet
grey laces drag under her feet
pink raincoat tied over her pajamas
patterned with cows fleeing the moon

Laura, where are you going? I ask
To sleep at Nora's   she says

She leaves the house
clutching her cell phone like a bludgeon
ducks through the door
in case spiders are hanging from the frame

My ex was naked,

wandering through
the dark downstairs.
Moonlight snuck
through the window
and I saw the tattered
clumps of hair
across his chest,
and how his penis
hung between
his legs like a broken
worm. I hadn't
seen him since
1989. He'd never
been in this house,
but I knew him
at once, the way
he stood as if
held taut by a string
from somewhere
above. I said,
"Jake, get out."
He nodded once,
then backed into
the room behind
the linen closet
I've never seen
before, although
Brian and I have lived
here for thirty years.
Old houses give up
their secrets slowly,
after midnight,
in the dark.

A Surefire Cure for Insomnia

For Sharon

A girl lived in a cottage in the woods
with three hundred hamsters
and the hamsters gathered
in a great congregation
muzzle to rump, flank to flank
and formed a rug of living fur.

The girl lay down and the hamsters,
moving as one beast
carried her outside to a patch
of clover and wild strawberries
and she lounged on their massed bodies
and ate fruit.

And a bear came and scooped her up
and carried her away
past the margin of the forest
past the village where light flickered
in the baker's shop and the smell
of bread infused the street.

And he carried her to the seaside
and laid her in the sand,
still warm from yesterday's sun.
The moon glittered the sea
and waves arched their necks
and galloped onto the strand.

Shorebirds covered her with their wings
their breasts puffed like pillows.
An osprey stood sentry,
a scream hushed in his throat
waiting to be launched
if she should cry out.

I Bear a Baby Again

My body splits open
right here in our bed
and I give birth

to a child who is
half-boy, half-caterpillar.
His body is covered

with fuzz and so small
he fits into my palm.
I nestle him against

the curve of my throat.
An inchworm of a child.
He wiggles up my neck

and kisses my cheek,
his kiss so quick
and cold a snowflake

might have grazed
my face. I wake and
tell you and we

both laugh, the bed
quivering beneath us,
but when I shut

my eyes I still feel
his small green shape
curled in my hand.

When My Brother Lost His Mind

And this was Wayne. My baby brother.
The smartest kid at Fairfield High
with perfect SATs, who beat me

every day at chess for two years straight
then rigged the pinball games at Mel's Arcade
so he could play all night for free.

I didn't know his thoughts began
to zing and flash like neon balls
bounced in a metal box before

they disappeared down dark holes.
At my wedding in June he fainted
because he thought my bridegroom

was the devil, then stripped off his clothes
on Bleecker Street because Satan
had wired them for sound

and was sending signals back home
to Hell. Even his teeth turned traitor,
drilling voices into his brain.

The night they took him to Bellevue
I dreamed he called my name three times,
Wayne's voice so sad and strange

he sounded like The Grateful Dead album
he dropped to shock the demons out
then cried each time the needle

jumped its groove and skittered
back to play the broken place
over and over again.

Wayne slept in his car

for weeks before he lost it
on Q Street. The Voices whispered misdirection.
Down by the canal, they suggested, *Wisconsin Avenue
outside the Russian Embassy*, and warned
that Putin and Wayne's old math teacher Mr. Gaffney
were now in league

and tormenting him with microwaves.
That was before the cops arrested him for vagrancy.
D.C. streets are no place for people like your brother,
the judge told his sister, so she took him home
to sleep on her couch. The next morning
they went to Blue Plains to search

vast fields of random cars
impounded by the city. Two days later he took off for Texas
with Mr. Gaffney and Putin in hot pursuit. And Wayne's
sister remembered how when they were children
they played badminton for hours summer nights,
the birdies fantastic moths

sailing through the failing light,
until Wayne's strokes became so wild
and strange they had to stop, the birdies lost
to corners of the roof where they lay staring
like eyes usurped by separate visions
only Wayne could see.

What no one will tell you,

how death, and love, and sex are all the same,
I wish to speak about plainly, without metaphor,
which might cloud your vision, like the cicadas
that filled the air the year my sister Barbara died

and you couldn't see past their plump brown bodies
rising over sidewalk and lawn. Our small brains can't
grasp this, the sameness, only how I sat on the front
steps for hours when I heard about Barbara, because

I lost my keys and could not get into the house, how
I shook like an insect trying to break free of its skin
and watched a plague of cicadas climb out of their holes
for a frenzy of sex after they left their husks and rose

into the air. How birds and squirrels feasted, and
you fingered the crisp abandoned shapes, holding
them with careful hands so not to crush their eye
ridges and stiff diaphanous wings, then ran to empty

your bladder behind the azaleas, which weren't in bloom
because it was August, the sound of cicadas droned
like the seaside, but there was no water and the grass
was brown, dying from heat and the brown carcasses

perched on their tips. Now I hear my cousin Bruce has
lymphoma and his wife Ellen has a melanoma which
has spread, and I remember how we got together every
year, Barbara, Wayne, Sharon and I, with the cousins,

Bruce, Stewart and Matt, and Billy and Beth, for vacations,
Bar Mitzvahs and such. How when Sharon was three, I held
her, danced and sang, *Sher-ree, Sher-air-airy, bay-ay-by*, and
Stewart teased me because I was so short and couldn't sing.

Now Beth has had both breasts removed, and Barbara
is dead. You are young, and in love, and don't understand
the sameness I'm trying to tell you about, how browness
will slide into your life when you are unaware, how cicadas

will slip from their skin and rise into the air when they are sated and ready to die, but now it's June, the front door is propped open and we sit together on the glider and swing, and the grass is quiet and green.

At Daniel's Bar Mitzvah

Laura, just turned seven,
pulled a squishy ball

painted like a bloodshot eye
out of her pocket, and when

the Bar Mitzvah boy marched
up and down the aisle

carrying the Torah,
Laura reached out and

touched the scroll
with the eyeball, and

kissed it, for a blessing.
Thus the Holy Eyeball

was born. It lived
in Laura's closet with tutus,

shawls and a trumpet.
When our house burned

down in 2006, the Eyeball,
its blessing still intact,

was unhurt. And when
I had cancer

and survived that too,
the Eyeball was still there,

dispensing beneficence.
(It's still there now.)

The Grandmother Gene

Sun is butter on my mother's face,
spills like apple juice over Becky's
highchair, down her front. Her black curls,
sticky with breakfast, stick out

every which way, gilded with Cheerios.
My mother also sports a Cheerio, a jaunty
stowaway, half hidden under a curl.
My daughter and my mother poke out

their tongues, wave them like crazy flags.
Brian clicks off the slide projector,
pats the machine like a geriatric friend.
Becky has just turned twenty-two,

Skypes her British boyfriend every night
planning her trip to London.
Three weeks later I get an email
from East Anglia. *Mom, don't have*

a heart attack but I used your Visa card
for a pregnancy test. Don't worry.
It's not for me. I bought it for a friend.
I believe her, of course.

I write, *Thanks for the warning.*
You're always so good to your friends.
I sit back, measure sugar into my tea.
I let my heart rate slow.

I'll never tell her how it pounded,
six beats—worry,
three beats—fear,
one beat—joy.

VI

November 1st

A thought drops from my brain then
founders, already I have forgotten
the quest, stranded halfway between
bedroom and den, why I set out

down the hall with such purpose,
my hands reaching for something
whose shape tingles my fingertips
but I cannot, cannot, remember

what it was I needed so urgently,
the sting gone out of my step, I
wander into the living room
and stare out the French windows,

we were so pleased how they brought
the outside in, and I study leaves,
how the tree has flung them
every which way, a tumult of yellow

and brown spattered by black spots
that Brian says is a fungus that will
kill the tree unless we sweep all dead
leaves away, the old infecting the new,

come spring. Aunt Norma died last night.
She was 95. She woke every morning
at 5 am and cried, because she was
not dead yet. The ash, the birch,

the sycamore conspire, drop their leaves
all at once. Even the wind is a tease, blowing
from every direction, leaves muddle in the air,
uncertain where to go or which way to fall.

Elegy

My mother's bones slip into mine
when I lie in bed. Feet crossed at the ankles,
arms behind my head. I picture her
lying just like this when she was ill.
As if waiting, at the pool side, at her ease.
Pneumonia, they told her in August
at the Doc in the Box at Valley View
half a mile from her house.
By October she began to say,
I wish my back didn't hurt so much.
Then Dr. Blake at Presbyterian
said, *Lung cancer.* My girls were tiny then,
believed us when we told them
Santa Claus would come to us in Dallas
that year. At midnight I got out of bed
and drove to the hospital. She was awake,
the first time since we'd arrived.
I held her hand. She couldn't speak
but she could look. At 4 I left
and went back to bed. My legs crossed,
my arms folded behind my head.
The nurse called at dawn.
Did I want to come? I said, *No.*
If I waited to see if each breath
was her last I thought I might die too.
Her mouth hanging open, slack.
As if she wished to suck something in,
or something wanted out.

Outside GWU Medical School
on Valentine's Day

The student bobbed when he walked,
but held the flower pot steady
as a surgical instrument. His white coat,
thrown open, flapped back in the wind.
The orchid nodded on its stalk.
He gazed at the purple petals
as if they shared some secret bond.
Was it for his sweetheart? His mom?
Or destined to bloom in the spot
of sun that tiles his desk,
Bates Guide to Physical Diagnosis
open to page two ninety-six,
the pulmonary exam, a diagram of lungs—
the bronchial tree branching downward,
bronchioles filling each lobe
with their minuscule blooms.

You were not

my twin although I dreamed you were when we were ten &
in my dream we looked exactly the same even though you were a boy & I
was a girl & we did not lie out on the grass summer evenings & you didn't
tell me your stories & when your guinea pig had pups you didn't give me
the biggest one & teach me three secret words in a language only guinea
pigs understand

& in ninth grade you didn't move to Michigan & your father
never grew apples & corn when he wasn't at the University & we didn't
write a novel together sending chapters back & forth from Norwalk to Ann
Arbor & when you were in high school through some bizarre coincidence
you never met my future lover James who also lived in Michigan & took
the bus with you to D.C. where you both marched for peace

& when I was seventeen I didn't take a train halfway across
the country to visit you & you never showed me how corn tasted like
honey when you chewed it raw off the cob or how when the sky turned
black we could slip off our clothes & go skinny dipping in the duck pond
& the water was so warm & thick it felt like night's tongue

& when we were all seniors in college & I was living
in Vermont with James in a trailer south of campus & James said you
couldn't stay with us even though you hitch-hiked from so far away to
see me & we both knew he was jealous & I didn't contradict him & you
didn't scream you would never speak to me again & I didn't believe you

& ten years later you didn't recognize my sister Barbara
in Minneapolis & run across Woodmont Street & scribble your phone
number on the back of a grocery receipt & say *tell Ellen to call me* & when
Barbara gave it to me I did not roll the paper until it was as small & bitter
as a grapefruit seed before I threw it away

Alternate Sonnet, for my Sisters

1. barbara's liver begins to fail. i ask my father
    should i fly to california?
2. *no* he says. *i'll call you when it's time to come.*
3. she dies that night.
4. i'm the oldest sister now.
5. barbara has acute myeloid leukemia in '84. she's 36.
6. sharon donates bone marrow to barbara.
    it's a perfect match.
7. i have leukemia in '09. i'm 59.
8. we both have bone marrow transplants
    but not at the same time.
9. the chance of survival is 50%.
10. sharon's bone marrow doesn't match mine.
11. when barbara dies sharon goes to bed for a month.
12. countdown: 3 sisters   2 transplants   1 death
13. (   ) in this line there is nothing
14. when i was a child i thought when we got old we'd all live
    together in manhattan and keep cats.

The Cards

Carl shut himself in the bathroom of Dorm A,
warding off our kisses. Kathy and I pressed
the wooden panels, taunted, *come out, come out.*

Carl said he didn't know if he liked girls or boys.
I thought if he could feel my lips, pillow himself
against my breasts, he would choose *girls.*

Bryce was Carl's roommate, David's friend.
I taught them how to knit, three boys and me
sitting on my dorm bed, knits and purls twisted

and uneven as anybody's fate. I slept with Bryce
but it was Carl I loved. Tall Carl, who dyed
his hair half-red, half-black. He laid out his cards.

This is your past. This is your future.
This is what covers you. This is
what crosses you. This is what crowns you.

The Empress. Fortune's Wheel.
The Judgment.
The Queen of Cups. The World.

After winter break, Carl came back coy, told me
he'd discovered it was *boys.* We reshuffled. Bryce
fell for Kathy. David slept with me, then dictated

the end of my séances with Carl. Years later,
someone gives my Becky tarot cards.
Carl, when I Google you nothing comes up.

I lay out the cards. *This is your past.*
This is your future. This is what covers you.
This is what crosses you. This is what crowns you.

I turn over The Priestess. The Hanged Man.
The Magician.
Fortune's Wheel. The Fool.

Mourning Uncle Howard

When Uncle Howard died his spirit drifted toward
Heaven but Jews don't believe in Heaven

so he disappeared into those high feathery clouds
clustered over Penobscot Bay.

Mother said one year it got so cold the Bay froze over.
Do you miss Maine? I asked. We sat on the sun porch of her

Dallas home and watched the thunderstorm roll in. *No,* she said.
I'm done with cold. I never want to be that cold again.

At seventy-eight Aunt Norma painted the ships in Belfast Harbor.
They yanked at their anchors like colts tethered in an icy field.

Look, Ellen, Aunt Norma said. *Look at the noses of the ships.
The tide pulls and pulls until they all face the same way.*

In '56 Howard sold the junkyard, bought a farm a few miles up
Route 1 in Searsport. The horses raised and lowered their muzzles

like old men davening in the back of the shul. *Who ever heard
of a Jewish horse farmer?* asked Uncle Joe.

Do you miss riding? I asked Aunt Norma.
Oh, yes, she said. *I remember what fun it was galloping*

*past the second field into the woods with Howard.
Galloping and laughing. A long time ago when we were sixty.*

I took my girls to the second field to pick wild blueberries.
The path was so overgrown we could hardly find our way.

The pump broke, and water from the old spring bubbled up
and bubbled up until the whole bottom of the field was lost.

Kaffeeklatsch

Judy, Jill, and I hover over coffee.
We shake rain off our coats, take out
notebooks and write. This is our ritual.

It is dark at our table outside Starbucks.
I sip my latte, Judy, a frappuccino,
Jill, a red eye. We hover over coffee

while the streetlight bleeds gray
into October air. We fill notebook
after notebook. This is our ritual.

The sparrows won't come to the sidewalk
table after sunset. We write *Confinement*
or *Eye in the Sky* and sip coffee.

Later we lay down our pens and talk,
preen broken feathers, chatter
and coo. This is our ritual.

My blood counts have dropped; Judy
has an ulcer on her left foot, Jill's medication
is wrong, she shakes, cries. Coffee

cannot cure her. We hold her hands,
stir sugar, cream into her drink.
Judy, Jill and I hover over coffee.
Cherish the taste. This is our ritual.

Little Kathy

It was a joke between us.
Kathy and I were the same size—
and a ten-year old child is taller than me.

I was at a party and the hostess,
a girl called Zoe, said, *Oh, I know Kathy,*
Kathy Gray? I saw her Tuesday.

And even in my dream
I remembered the day Brian told me
Kathy was dead. I was in the hospital,

I was the one who was deathly ill,
not her, and Brian leaned over the bed
and took my hand and told me.

I was dopey with morphine
and couldn't cry, but it seemed like
tears were pooling in front of my face

and drifting around the room,
like we were suddenly in outer space
and what could not be true was true.

In my dream I told Zoe, *It can't be Kathy,*
She's been my dear friend forever,
but she passed away years ago.

Zoe said, *She's not dead.* Shame burned
through me. I must be a terrible friend.
I hadn't spoken to Kathy since 2009.

And I remembered Suburban Hospital—
how Brian pressed my palm between
his hands and I felt his breath on my cheek.

Old Bones

crowd our bedroom,
rattle and clack, an orchestra
ground to ivory by long
sojourn beneath the earth.
See their faces? Sockets bare,
skulls, empty coffers,
gilded and jeweled
but rifled long ago,
marrow sucked away,
hollow as sparrow bones.

Oh, love, I envy them.
My sorrow will not fly away.
We are conjoined,
despair and I, grown
more close than joint and sinew.
Look away. I would not have you see,
as I do, stars reduced
to pinholes pricked in sooty copper.
Even night is no longer honest black.

You breathe beside me, a rhythmic
slap that bears you into sleep.
My breasts round against your back.
Beloved, you are my harbor,
tropical port whose honeyed air
hints almonds and oranges,
home beyond death.

The frenzied muscle
that thumps and mourns
quiets inside my chest.
Sanctuary, I cry
to the fierce presence
that harrows me.

You float away from me.
I cast my net into the dreaming sea,
hope for nuggets of emerald and topaz,
true stars, your buoyant heart.

When My Father Died

we were right there
goodbye sweetheart she said
   mother's voice a girl's voice
so intimate
  I thought
  I shouldn't be listening

  and backed away
but in the hall
  I shook and
my shoulders heaved
  she said *ellen we mustn't*
  give way like this

  she smelled of
snowdrops
  her hair coiled
into a perfect bun
  held with a single
  pearl clip

  her shoulder
pressed into mine
  and her hand
perched on my arm
  and quivered
  like a winter bird

Flatsy

When she was nine my sister Barbara said
she dreamed she'd been flattened into a picture,
squashed into crayon marks on white paper
and a witch tore her into pieces and threw her
out the window of an airplane and I pictured
Barbara's face flying out a window into the sky.

That was when I had a doll named Flatsy,
plastic, but flat as a paper doll. I wondered
what it would be like to be part girl, part picture.
I could never forgive Flatsy for that, how she
would disappear when you turned her
sideways, how she had no room inside for bones,

or blood, how a witch could rip her in two.
I threw Flatsy away after Barbara died
of leukemia, borrowed my mother's
sewing scissors and snipped old Flatsy
into a dozen pieces and buried her
under the flagstones lining the back walk.

We never did scatter my sister's ashes,
or my mother's, or father's when cancer
took them, but laid them neatly in the same plot
in South Dallas. Mother was the last to go,
of lung disease, in '95. At her Unveiling

I sat at her graveside and waited to feel
three dimensional again. It was pleasant there,
so cool under the pink feathered blossoms
of mimosa trees, but there were no hills to ease
your eyes. No curves roll the earth's body
in that resting place. It's like that in Texas, so flat.

Monday Night, 11:30pm

Spooned in bed
with you, your arm
a careless weight
across my middle,
your breath,
a muted snore,
hums in my ear.
This is bread and butter
love, served with brisket,
or chuck, or some other
homely cut, braised
in a slow oven,
then placed on the table
in its crown
of carrots and herbs.

At Rosh Hashanah Services

I felt space open between yesterday
and today. I sat in the last pew. And
I could not see Cantor Lydia's face.
All I saw was a blur. As if she too

stood outside time. When I was sick
with cancer in '09 it seemed someone
knocked a hole in Now and I might leak
out. So close I could stick my arm through.

I thought it might be a blessing to lose
my face, release it like an injured bird
into the Baltimore sky.
Crows roosted in the tulip trees

outside the hospital window, a blur
of black wings.

La Petite Mort

the little death

if that is so why have I feared
its big brother all these years
la grande mort
all sensation
coming together for one grand blowout
then the quiet
that will not end

you will not be there with me

but I will not forget
how you have burned
the deep poles of my body
cold and hot

until my skin flows with a current
that quivers toes   fingertips
fevers with an ague
that makes my nails chime

I did not know before you came
how my womb could open
like a thirsty child
calling   more water
more *petite morte*

Yartzeit

Father's hair never turns gray.
The back grows bald
and his forehead nibbles
his hairline away. I wonder
if he has rubbed it off lying
all those days in the ICU.
His thoughts bubble
out of control, his brain
goes incandescent with fantasy.
How graciously he greets me.
He thinks he's lounging
in the American Embassy in Vilnius.
The next day he announces
he's leaving and pulls off his tubes.
He stands up and falls on his head.
Blood leaks in his brain and
the bubble goes dark.

Mother lives two more years
almost to the day. She eats alone,
dines on cottage cheese
and prunes, mislays
her hearing aid.
Her neighbor invites
her to the symphony,
but she can't hear the melody.
Lung cancer reels her in,
delivers her to the hospice wing.
Her heart rebels, refuses to stop.
Radiation fails to diminish
her hair. Her chest tightens,
her breath slows.
Silver waves fall over her shoulder
and soften her hospital gown.
I finger-comb her curls.

About the Author

Ellen Aronofsky Cole is a poet, actress, and teaching artist. Her publications include her chapbook Prognosis, published by Finishing Line Press. Her poems have appeared in The Bellevue Literary Review, Little Patuxent Review, Potomac Review, The Innisfree Poetry Journal, The Washington Post Magazine, Bogg: A Journal of Contemporary Writing, and Pulse: Voices from the Heart of Medicine, and elsewhere. Her article "My Life as a (Fake) Patient," was published in The New England Journal of Medicine. Ellen works as a medical actress at GWU School of Medicine and other medical schools, taking the part of the patients in role-plays with medical students. She lives in Silver Spring, Maryland with her husband Brian, and a small, feisty parrot named Haiku.

Other Recent Titles from Mayapple Press:

Monica Wendel, *English Kills and other poems*
Paper, 70pp, $15.95
ISBN 978-1-936419-84-5

Charles Rafferty, *Something an Atheist Might Bring Up at a Cocktail Party*, 2018
Paper, 40pp, $14.95
ISBN 978-1-936419-83-8

David Lunde, *Absolute Zero*, 2018
Paper, 82pp, $16.95 plus s&h
ISBN 978-1-936419-80-7

Jan Minich, *Wild Roses*, 2017
Paper, 100pp, $16.95 plus s&h
ISBN 978-1-936419-77-7

John Palen, *Distant Music*, 2017
Paper, 74pp, $15.95 plus s&h
ISBN 978-1-936419-74-6

Eleanor Lerman, *The Stargazer's Embassy*, 2017
Paper, 310pp, $18.95 plus s&h
ISBN 978-936419-73-9

Dicko King, *Bird Years*, 2017
Paper, 80pp, $14.95 plus s&h
ISBN 978-936419-69-2

Eugenia Toledo, tr. Carolyne Wright, *Map Traces, Blood Traces /
Trazas de Mapas, Trazas de Sangre*, 2017
Paper, 138pp, $16.95 plus s&h
ISBN 978-936419-60-9

Eric Torgersen, *In Which We See Our Selves: American Ghazals*, 2017
Paper, 44pp, $14.95 plus s&h
ISBN 978-936419-72-2

Toni Ortner, *A White Page Demands Its Letters*, 2016
Paper, 40pp, $14.95 plus s&h
ISBN 978-936419-70-8

Rivka Basman Ben-Haim, tr. Zelda Newman, *The Thirteenth Hour*
Paper, 94pp, $15.95 plus s&h
ISBN 978-936419-71-5

Nola Garrett, *Ledge*, 2016
Paper, 94pp, $15.95 plus s&h
ISBN 978-936419-68-5

For a complete catalog of Mayapple Press publications, please visit our website at *www.mayapplepress.com*. Books can be ordered direct from our website with secure on-line payment using PayPal, or by mail (check or money order). Or order through your local bookseller.